Pressing In
It's Worth It All

GLORIA COPELAND

KENNETH
COPELAND
PUBLICATIONS

Unless otherwise noted, all scripture is from the *King James Version* of the Bible.

Scripture quotations marked *The Amplified Bible* are from *The Amplified Bible, Old Testament* © 1965, 1987 by the Zondervan Corporation. *The Amplified New Testament* © 1958, 1987 by The Lockman Foundation. Used by permission.

Scripture quotations marked *New International Version* are from *The Holy Bible, New International Version*, © 1973, 1978, 1984 by the International Bible Society. Used by permission of Zondervan Publishing House.

Pressing In—It's Worth It All

ISBN-10 0-88114-842-3   30-0528
ISBN-13 978-0-88114-842-8

15 14 13 12 11 10   10 9 8 7 6 5

Kenneth Copeland Publications
Fort Worth, TX 76192-0001

For more information about Kenneth Copeland Ministries, call 800-600-7395 or visit www.kcm.org.

Pressing In—
It's Worth It All

by Gloria Copeland

What does it take to be a winner? Everyone wants to know the answer to that question. We all want to win. But when it comes right down to it, few of us are willing to pay the price.

One day I heard an Olympic athlete describe how hard she had worked for the opportunity to compete in the Olympic Games. She was telling what it took for her to win the gold medal.

Olympic athletes don't just wake up one morning and say, "Hey! I think I'll be in the Olympics today." They train for years to get there. Some of them train most of their lives.

They get out of bed every morning to run. They run in the cold. They run in the rain. They run no matter what—whether they want to or not. This woman said there were times when she pushed herself so hard she became physically ill. But even then, she refused to stop running.

That woman was determined to win.

She had decided years earlier she was going to go for a gold medal—no matter what the cost. She was stretching and straining to win it, pushing forward with the kind of force that moves every obstacle out of the way.

That kind of force is what it takes to be a winner—not just physically but also spiritually. Jesus said this in Matthew 11:12, "And from the days of John the Baptist until now the kingdom of heaven suffereth violence, and the violent take it by force."

In this verse, Jesus wasn't talking about going to heaven. He was talking about taking hold of the kingdom of God on this earth—actually possessing the promised blessings like healing, prosperity and peace.

You can have those kingdom blessings now. But it's not easy—you have to take them by force.

Faith: A Violent Force

Most people don't see faith as a violent force. But spiritually speaking, it is! Paul said, "*Fight* the good fight of faith..." (1 Timothy 6:12).

Faith is aggressive. It uses the Word of God as a weapon and brings down every stronghold of unbelief and every demonic obstacle in its path!

You must become spiritually aggressive if you want to walk in the supernatural. You have to do it by faith using the Word of God or you won't do it at all.

People who don't know about aggressive faith waste a great deal of time. When they find themselves in a difficult situation, they often just sit back and wait for God to rescue them.

But you won't get anywhere just waiting for God to do everything. He's already given you the blood of Jesus and the power of the Holy Spirit. He won't do your part! As one minister says, "The Holy Spirit is your helper and if you don't do what you're supposed to, He doesn't have anything to help."

So, don't just sit there—do something! Fight the good fight of faith! Put the Word of God in your heart and in your mouth every day. Get aggressive. Make it your lifestyle. The Apostle Paul did. He said: "I have fought a good fight, I have finished my course, I have kept the faith" (2 Timothy 4:7).

I'll tell you something else: No matter how much you know or how long you've been in the walk of faith, the basics don't change.

Ken and I have never encountered a problem from which God didn't deliver us. On the other hand, we've never been in a situation that didn't require us to walk by faith and do all the basic things we learned many years ago. It has never changed. It never will.

The faith-filled lifestyle is ordained by God and is

the only walk that works. It works by principles and laws that God put into operation.

To live this lifestyle, faith must be in two places—in your heart *and* in your mouth.

If faith is only in your heart, then it's not expressing itself and therefore, can't be applied to the natural realm around you. When you're in the midst of a struggle, save yourself some time—just look at the opening right under your nose. That's usually the answer to "What have I been doing wrong?" You've been talking the problem instead of the answer. On the other hand, if it's only in your mouth and not in your heart, then there's no real force behind it because faith *comes* from the heart.

Faith is the only force that will change natural things or natural circumstances. It is the only force that can apply itself to the natural realm to change or move a mountain.

But you won't have that powerful faith if you're influenced by the world's goods and feeding on its information. The source you draw from determines what is going to be on the inside of you and what will come out.

You may know God's promises. But if you don't take the time to put God's Word in your heart—even though you might be able to "say" the right things—your words won't come out in power to move your mountain.

Maybe you are feeding on God's Word, and yet

the situation you face still seems impossible. I know it's hard to speak words of faith when you're facing such hard times. But don't stop feeding on the only thing that can change your situation. Remember, you were born again so that you could accomplish hard things—impossible things!

I think it was a great blessing that Ken and I were in our own impossible situation financially when we first began to hear the word of faith. (I didn't think it was a blessing then, of course, but I do now!) Our finances were minus zero at that point in our lives. We didn't have anything but our debts.

We were so desperate we *had* to believe God. It was the hardest believing we ever did because we didn't know very much.

It was easier for us to believe our way out of the $6 million deficit we faced a few years ago than it was to believe for the little amount we needed back then. But do you know, when it came down to it—when we needed to receive that $6 million—we did exactly the same thing we did the first time we ever believed for grocery money.

We fought the fight of faith. We got aggressive with the Word.

Press In

The fact is, if you want to lay hold of the authority

of God and walk in the supernatural, you can't do it from your easy chair. You have to press in. Jesus said, "The law and the prophets were until John: since that time the kingdom of God is preached, and every man presseth into it" (Luke 16:16). Paul wrote, "...I press on to lay hold of (grasp) and make my own, that for which Christ Jesus (the Messiah) has laid hold of me and made me His own" (Philippians 3:12, *The Amplified Bible*).

Press in. That's as important a concept for us today as it was in Moses' time. Moses pressed in the Spirit. He wanted to see God's glory. I'm that way too. I'd want to see God's glory even if I knew I wouldn't live through it.

That heart cry to know God keeps us pressing in to lay hold of more of His kingdom each day of our lives. It pushes us toward the goal of knowing Jesus and finishing the race God has set before us.

If you want to go on with God like Moses and Paul did, then that desire is going to have to become the cry of your heart. Paul's heart cry to know the Lord made him determined not to quit. He was determined to press on until he laid hold of every task the Lord had for him.

One day while on a journey to bring persecution to the Church, Paul was laid hold of by Jesus. The *King James Version* of the Bible says he was "apprehended" by Jesus. From that time until the day he went to be with the Lord, Paul was committed to fulfilling the calling for which he was apprehended. He would not quit early. Even with his intense desire to be with Christ in heaven, Paul was willing to stay on earth knowing the need of believers to whom he ministered (Philippians 1:21-26).

Finish Your Race

Just as Paul ran his race—his life's course—there's also a race marked out for you. God has charted that course and only you can run it. Only by pressing in to win your race will you see the fullness of God's provision in your life.

And let me add: God didn't choose you for that race based on your ability, intellect, or anything you could do in the natural. He planned to empower you with *His* ability to do the job that He prepared for you. It's in the weakness of your natural ability that He can show Himself strong. Don't be deceived into thinking someone else can run your race. No one can run another person's race.

If we knew the races marked out for everyone ahead of time, we'd probably choose other people to run them. We would think, *Not that person—they'll never make it!*

Let me tell you how God picks people for their tasks: He looks at the heart. He doesn't always choose from the greatest universities. It's difficult for Him to use those who think they can handle situations in their own wisdom and strength. "For the eyes of the Lord run to and fro throughout the whole earth, to show himself strong in the behalf of them whose heart is perfect toward him" (2 Chronicles 16:9). In this verse, *perfect* means "devoted, consecrated, dedicated, loyal, faithful."

I want to tell you something that will take a lot of pressure off you and will release faith action: *The race you have been chosen to run is impossible to finish on your own.* Everything we're chosen to do is impossible because God wants it done by faith.

It took a lot of pressure off me when I realized God never intended for us to know how to do what He tells us to do. He never intended for me or Ken to know how to go on television. He intended to do it through us. *He* knows how! We just have to do what we're told.

Our part is to maintain our fellowship with Him. His part is to do the work through us. When you're in God, you're in over your head all the time. Get used to it and keep on pressing in.

No Time to Hesitate

If there was ever a generation that needed to press in to the things of God, it's our generation. I believe we are living in the last days. I believe Jesus is coming soon and that helps me to keep my life focused on Him.

In recent times, the Church has not given enough attention to Jesus' soon return. The fact that He could come at any moment ought to be foremost in our hearts. We ought to preach it to people and share it.

The Scripture says our hope of His return purifies us (1 John 3:3). People wouldn't pour so much energy into material things if they thought Jesus would be coming back in less than a decade. They wouldn't be as carnal. They'd be pressing into the things of the Spirit and storing up heavenly rewards.

Now is our opportunity to do that! Our rewards, our rank, even our responsibilities in heaven will be determined by what we do here on earth. For a few brief years here, we have the opportunity to influence people around us—to let the character of the Lord Jesus Christ and the love of God flow out through us and reveal God to the world.

Just a few years and that opportunity will be gone. In the meantime, it's worth living for...and dying for. It's worth whatever sacrifices we have to make.

Go Ahead, Assert Yourself!

How do you get the kind of spiritual aggressiveness, the urgency it takes to lay hold of that opportunity?

First, you must determine your focus and spend time with God. The Apostle Paul said, "[For my determined purpose is] that I may know Him [that I may progressively become more deeply and intimately acquainted with Him..." (Philippians 3:10, *The Amplified Bible*).

Notice Paul didn't say, "One of my purposes is...." He said very specifically, "My *determined* purpose is...." I can promise you this: You won't be spiritually aggressive unless you determine to be. You'll let "...the cares of this world, and the deceitfulness of riches, and the lusts of other things" get in your way (Mark 4:19).

I need to warn you, that determination to spend time with God will run headlong into a busy life. To stay on course, you will have to bring your flesh under the rule of your spirit and be willing to simplify your life.

I discovered this as I was honoring a prophecy the Lord gave through Kenneth E. Hagin on the importance of communing with the Father:

> Don't take up all your time with natural things...give your spirit opportunity to feed upon the Word of God...to commune with the Father above and build yourself up on your most holy faith. It doesn't take a lot of time, just an hour or two out of 24. Just pay a tithe of your time unto Me, saith the Lord, and all will be well. Your life will be changed. It will be empowered and you will be a mighty force for God.

I never was a great person of prayer. I'm really still

not like some people I know. But some years ago I decided I'd pray at least an hour a day.

Can I tell you what you probably already know? When my alarm went off, I'd get up...sometimes. Other times, I'd think—and I know it was the devil—*Look how dark it is outside. It's so cold this morning. You don't want to get up.*

Sometimes in those first few weeks, I'd agree with the devil: "That's right, I don't," and I'd go back to sleep. But I kept at it, and kept at it and kept at it. Eventually it became a habit with me. Now I don't turn over and go back to sleep anymore.

You see, your body must be trained by your spirit. It will get up. My body never says to me anymore, "It's so cold outside. It's so dark...." My body is so used to getting up in the dark, it doesn't even think about it.

The tithe of my time to the Lord changed my life because I purposed in my heart to not be lazy, draw back, hold back or sit down. I purposed not to spend my life wasting time on natural things. I set goals that I was going to do every day.

It wasn't easy. When I started I could hardly pray for even five minutes—that was a long time for me. But I stayed with it. Seizing the kingdom isn't easy. God doesn't say it will be easy, but He does say it will be worth it.

Hard times demand that you take time to be with the Lord—time to put your flesh down and stir your faith up.

Once you have determined to know God—to become more deeply and intimately acquainted with Him—your second step is to spend time with Him. That's always the bottom line, isn't it? Whenever we start pressing in, desiring to win more victories in the Spirit, desiring more power, we're always directed back to that precious time with Him.

Look again at what Paul said, "[For my determined purpose is] that I may know Him...And that I may in that same way come to know the power outflowing from His resurrection..." (Philippians 3:10, *The Amplified Bible*).

Think about it. If you spend an hour with God every day, that's 365 hours a year. Don't you think coming into His presence for an hour every day will do something for your life? Even if you just spent 15 minutes a day, that would be 90 hours a year of prayer and time with Him. An hour is just what the Lord led *me* to do. Follow your own heart. But see to it that you give the Father time to impart His strength into you.

Do you want Jesus' resurrection power to flow in your life? Then get to know Him! The more you fellowship with Him, the more you're going to look like Him, act like Him and talk like Him.

That's not surprising, really. It's a fact of life. When you spend time around strong people, you begin to take on their way of talking, thinking and even their mannerisms. When you spend time with Jesus, you'll do exactly the same thing.

So, if you spend your time watching secular television and filling your mind with the world's news, what do you think will happen? You'll end up being like the world and living in fear instead of faith.

What you give your attention to is what's going to be on the inside of you. And what's inside you will determine the outcome of your situation. Your future is stored up in your heart. (See Matthew 12:34-35, *New International Version.)*

Press Toward the Mark

Once your focus and your fellowship is in place, press. To *press* means "to act with steady force or weight; to be insistent about; to exert pressure." It means "to go forward with energetic or determined effort."

Paul said, "I press toward the mark for the prize of the high calling of God in Christ Jesus" (Philippians 3:14).

To be a winner, you press. You press in to what God has called you to do. You don't float into it. You press forward by faith, believing the Word of God and not what natural circumstances say.

No matter where you are today in your spiritual growth, you won't progress without pressing. Remember what I said about those Olympic athletes? They know what it means to press toward a goal. They know what it means to put everything else aside and live like winners.

If natural people with natural discipline and desire to reach a goal can do that, certainly you and I can do it in the Spirit! We can do it with the power of the Holy Ghost in us and the Word of God in our hearts and in our mouths. We can press until we finish the race God has called us to run.

Remember, the natural world will always tell you that you can't do it—it's too big for you. You're too foolish. You're too weak. But God just says, *Do it, and I'll make up the difference.*

Stretch Toward the Finish Line

That means we stretch forward to the things in front of us. We bear down on the goal.

Paul was so intensely focused on pursuing the prize of his call in Christ that he would not allow himself to look anywhere but toward the goal. He ran, "forgetting those things which are behind, and reaching forth unto those things which are before..." (Philippians 3:13).

Paul never stopped stretching. When he was imprisoned, he wrote most of the New Testament. How was he able to do this? Look at Acts 20:22-24:

And now, behold, I go bound in the spirit unto Jerusalem, not knowing the things that shall befall me there: save that the Holy Ghost witnesseth in every city, saying that bonds and afflictions abide me. But none of these things move me, neither count I my life dear unto myself, so that I might finish my course with joy, and the ministry, which I have received of the Lord Jesus, to testify the gospel of the grace of God.

Paul could stretch toward the goal without distraction because he didn't count his life dear to himself. He had found something worth giving his life for. One day while I was reading this scripture the Lord impressed me, *Gloria, this is the key to your success spiritually. If you count your life dear unto yourself, you won't finish your race.*

Counting your life dear to yourself means that you've let the distractions of the age get hold of you. You concentrate on what *you* want and what *you* want to do—*your* happiness.

Jesus said if we would lose our lives for His sake, we would find them. That's life worth living. There's no peace in living like the world and going after things. But seek Him first and His righteousness, and all the other things will come to you.

The Joy of Winning

Paul knew where to look for his joy. He said he was going to "finish [his] course with joy." He was going to complete the ministry to which he had been called. He did not focus on his own life—his personal desires. He was going to finish his race and when he crossed the line there was going to be a smile on his face.

He intended not only to finish but to do it with joy. I like that. I too am not only going to finish my race and win but I'm going to enjoy it!

Do you see that we're not talking about a race where at the end we're going to drag up to the finish line depressed and despondent? We are talking about a race God intends for us to finish with joy.

Don't let the natural realm determine your level of courage or disappointment. The life of spirit beings is not sustained in the natural. A lot of our troubles are caused because our desires are incorrectly focused. Peace and joy, however, belong to those who keep their hearts full of God. So look in the right places for your joy.

Don't get distracted by anything—even legitimate things. If they have preeminence in your life, they are not right for you. One day each of us will stand before God. I personally don't think I will live out my natural life on earth. I expect Jesus to come before that happens. When I stand before the Lord, nothing will matter except that I finished my course.

Give It All You've Got

Don't misunderstand me. God has blessed Ken and me. We're not doing without anything. We're blessed and prosperous, but the desire and motivation of our hearts is to please God. It is to walk in what we are called to do and to finish our course. We feel it's worth giving our lives in order to obtain.

You see, according to 1 Corinthians 9:24, there is a prize that all who run may obtain. But the flesh must be brought into subjection in order to win that prize:

> Every man that striveth for the mastery is temperate in all things. Now they do it to obtain a corruptible crown; but we an incorruptible. I therefore so run, not as uncertainly; so fight I, not as one that beateth the air: But I keep under my body, and bring it into subjection: lest that by any means, when I have preached to others, I myself should be a castaway (1 Corinthians 9:25-27).

One translation says, "I reduce to slavery my body." We can't let our bodies rule us in this hour. We're going to have to walk in the spirit. We're going to have to crucify the flesh.

The things we turn down or accept determine the manifestation of the power of God in our lives. God's glory belongs to those who do not live after the flesh and who are no longer dominated by their bodies.

Before this age comes to a close, God is going to have a glorious Church—a people who refuse to live according to the dictates of the flesh or to be dominated by their bodies. He is going to have a Church that walks in His manifest glory.

Will You Pay the Price?

Here's the question: Do you and I want to be a part of that Church badly enough to run the race? Do we want it enough to pray and spend time in the Word instead of doing other things we could be doing—even good things?

I am one of those who love His appearing. I am believing for the Church to rise up and press in the spirit to get the things done that we need to do.

God is on a timetable. He's never late. And the Church is going to be ready. We're going to do what we're called to do.

Individuals may fall out of the race. You and I could fall out if we don't do the right things, if we don't do the things we know to do. But the Church is going to finish the race, and it's going to be on time. I want to be in that group and bring God glory.

The choice is yours. No one else can make it for you. Only you can determine in your heart, "My purpose is that I may know Him and I'm going to press and stretch and run the race He's called me to run."

You may think, *Well, what can I do? What God's called me to do couldn't be that important. It won't matter to people whether I do it or not. Nobody's life depends on it.*

That's not true. You can reach people no one else can reach. Noah was just one man. While his neighbors laughed, Noah kept building the ark. Despite the fact that no one had ever seen rain, Noah just kept obeying God.

His name is listed with the great men of faith in Hebrews 11. In fact, every person in Hebrews 11 who obtained a good report did it by faith.

The same chapter says God framed the worlds by faith. You'll have to walk by faith if you're going to finish. You'll have to get your heart and your mouth in line with God's Word if you're going to finish what you're called to do.

Travel Light

Once you've made the decision to finish your race, there's one other element of spiritual aggressiveness to put into motion. Patience.

Patience doesn't sound very aggressive, does it? But it is. In Hebrews 12:1-2 Paul says we are to run our race with patience and without encumbrance: "Wherefore seeing we also are compassed about with so great a cloud of witnesses, let us lay aside every weight, and the sin which doth so easily beset us, and let us run with patience the race that is set before us, looking unto Jesus the author and finisher of our faith...."

Think about those Olympic runners. Think of them pushing themselves to the limit, focusing on the goal, training themselves day after day—with what? With patience! In the Greek, that word means "steady continuance."

Patience means you don't quit. You keep doing what you know to do. Sometimes you may not see results for a while. But eventually, if you keep pressing, you'll get there. As Kenneth E. Hagin said, "God doesn't settle up every Saturday night, but He does settle up."

Weights and sin are two different things. But both of them must be removed if we're going to continue running.

Weights are things that pull you down into the natural realm when you ought to be soaring in the Spirit. So let go of whatever holds you back! Press into the Spirit and run.

Sin is revealed by God's Word and the Holy Spirit's conviction. You know when you have sinned. Confess it. Deal with it, so you can run. Lay it aside and get back on track.

Don't Get Distracted

As you lay aside weights and sin, resist distractions too. Don't allow the devil to draw your attention away. Just keep "looking unto Jesus." That's how you run this race. You can't focus on circumstances or your natural abilities. Keep your eyes on Jesus and His ability.

Peter walked on the water as long as he kept his eyes fixed on Jesus. When he began to look at the wind and the waves in the natural realm he began to sink.

Distraction can come from many directions. One of the most common tactics of the enemy is to trip you up with persecution. Don't let persecution throw you. In 2 Timothy 3:12 Paul wrote, "All that will live godly in Christ Jesus shall suffer persecution." It's just part of the package.

One day I became concerned thinking about the fact that nobody had been picking on us lately. "Ken, are we slipping?" I asked. "Are we not living godly? What is this?"

Just a few days later, we got a letter telling us all the things we did wrong and what heretics we were. I felt better after that.

Persecution is part of the package. Don't let it stop you. Don't let it distract you.

Jesus also warned us of the distractions of this age. The deceitfulness of riches and the lusts of other things can creep in and choke the Word and make it fruitless

(Mark 4:19). Right next to that verse in my Bible I've written the letters S-C-U-D. They stand for the phrase, "Satan Continuously Uses Distractions." He's always firing those SCUD missiles at you to discourage you and draw you off course.

"Hey," he'll whisper, "have you noticed you don't have any money? Have you noticed your body is in pain? Have you heard all the ugly things people are saying about you?"

Never Give Up

How do you fight distractions like that? Just "continue thou in the things which thou hast learned and hast been assured of, knowing of whom thou hast learned them" (2 Timothy 3:14).

It won't be the great revelation you haven't received yet that will cause you defeat. It will be failing to do what you already know to do. You won't come out of the hard place when the money shows up at the bank. You'll come out when God's power, anointing and faith show up inside you.

You'll come out of your hard situation only when God's Word gets so big inside you that you're not moved by what's in the bank. It may take a day or two for it to show up in the bank, but you'll get victory inside first. That never changes.

So whenever you reach a hard place, continue to do

what you know and you'll make it through just fine.

You've Got What It Takes

God's Word to you is "I will be with you." When Moses asked, "Who am I to go to Pharaoh?" God's answer was, "I will be with you." After Moses' death, God told Joshua the same thing: "I will be with thee: I will not fail thee, nor forsake thee. Be strong and of a good courage..." (Joshua 1:5-6).

Even if you get into trouble by your own thinking, God will honor you if you accept correction: "...whoever heeds correction is honored" (Proverbs 13:18, *New International Version).* Glory to God! If you press into His kingdom, stretching toward your prize, and remain correctable, He will make sure you stay headed in the right direction. He is with you and for you.

Do you wonder where your attention is? Watch your life. Watch what motivates you and what you're thinking about. Your words will follow your actions. So keep watch and don't let divine things lose out.

Don't be dismayed. Don't lose your courage. Do what you're called to do.

You have everything it takes to be a winner—everything you need to be part of the glorious, victorious end-time army of God. As Kenneth E. Hagin said in a prophecy God gave him in 1977, "You can be a part of that army if you want to be. Purpose in your heart that you'll not be lazy, that you'll not draw back, hold back or sit down. But purpose in your heart that you'll rise up and march forward and become on fire."

Get aggressive. Press in. Lay hold of the kingdom of God with every bit of force you can muster. That's the price you pay to win this race. But one thing is certain— the eternal victory you gain will be worth it all.

Prayer for Salvation and Baptism in the Holy Spirit

Heavenly Father, I come to You in the Name of Jesus. Your Word says, "Whosoever shall call on the name of the Lord shall be saved" (Acts 2:21). I am calling on You. I pray and ask Jesus to come into my heart and be Lord over my life according to Romans 10:9-10: "If thou shalt confess with thy mouth the Lord Jesus, and shalt believe in thine heart that God hath raised him from the dead, thou shalt be saved. For with the heart man believeth unto righteousness; and with the mouth confession is made unto salvation." I do that now. I confess that Jesus is Lord, and I believe in my heart that God raised Him from the dead.

I am now reborn! I am a Christian—a child of Almighty God! I am saved! You also said in Your Word, "If ye then, being evil, know how to give good gifts unto your children: HOW MUCH MORE shall your heavenly Father give the Holy Spirit to them that ask him?" (Luke 11:13). I'm also asking You to fill me with the Holy Spirit. Holy Spirit, rise up within me as I praise God. I fully expect to speak with other tongues as You give me the utterance (Acts 2:4). In Jesus' Name. Amen!

Begin to praise God for filling you with the Holy Spirit. Speak those words and syllables you receive—not in your own language, but the language given to you by the Holy Spirit. You have to use your own voice. God will not force you to speak. Don't be concerned with how it sounds. It is a heavenly language!

Continue with the blessing God has given you and pray in the spirit every day.

You are a born-again, Spirit-filled believer. You'll never be the same!

Find a good church that boldly preaches God's Word and obeys it. Become part of a church family who will love and care for you as you love and care for them.

We need to be connected to each other. It increases our strength in God. It's God's plan for us.

Make it a habit to watch the *Believer's Voice of Victory* television broadcast and become a doer of the Word, who is blessed in his doing (James 1:22-25).

About the Author

Gloria Copeland is a noted author and minister of the gospel whose teaching ministry is known throughout the world. Believers worldwide know her through Believers' Conventions, Victory Campaigns, magazine articles, teaching audios and videos, and the daily and Sunday *Believer's Voice of Victory* television broadcast, which she hosts with her husband, Kenneth Copeland. She is known for "Healing School," which she began teaching and hosting in 1979 at KCM meetings. Gloria delivers the Word of God and the keys to victorious Christian living to millions of people every year.

Gloria is author of the New York Times best-seller, *God's Master Plan for Your Life,* as well as numerous favorites, including *God's Will for You, Walk With God, God's Will Is Prosperity, Hidden Treasures* and *To Know Him.* She has also co-authored several books with her husband, including *Family Promises, Healing Promises* and the best-selling daily devotionals, *From Faith to Faith* and *Pursuit of His Presence.*

She holds an honorary doctorate from Oral Roberts University. In 1994, Gloria was voted Christian Woman of the Year, an honor conferred on women whose example demonstrates outstanding Christian leadership. Gloria is also the co-founder and vice president of Kenneth Copeland Ministries in Fort Worth, Texas.

Materials to Help You Receive Your Healing
by Gloria Copeland

Books

* And Jesus Healed Them All
  God's Prescription for Divine Health
  God's Will for Your Healing
* Harvest of Health
  Words That Heal (gift book with CD enclosed)

Audio Resources

Be Made Whole—Live Long, Live Healthy
God Is a Good God
God Wants You Well
Healing Confessions (CD and minibook)
Healing School

DVD Resources

Be Made Whole—Live Long, Live Healthy
Know Him As Healer

Books Available From
Kenneth Copeland Ministries

by Kenneth Copeland

*   A Ceremony of Marriage
     A Matter of Choice
     Blessed to Be a Blessing
     Covenant of Blood
     Faith and Patience—The Power Twins
*   Freedom From Fear
     Giving and Receiving
     Honor—Walking in Honesty, Truth and Integrity
     How to Conquer Strife
     How to Discipline Your Flesh
     How to Receive Communion
     In Love There Is No Fear
     Know Your Enemy
     Living at the End of Time—A Time of
         Supernatural Increase
     Love Letters From Heaven
     Love Never Fails
*   Mercy—The Divine Rescue of the Human Race
*   Now Are We in Christ Jesus
     One Nation Under God (gift book with CD enclosed)
*   Our Covenant With God
     Partnership—Sharing the Vision, Sharing the Grace
*   Prayer—Your Foundation for Success
*   Prosperity: The Choice Is Yours
     Rumors of War
*   Sensitivity of Heart
*   Six Steps to Excellence in Ministry
*   Sorrow Not! Winning Over Grief and Sorrow
*   The Decision Is Yours

* Available in Spanish

Books Co-Authored by Kenneth and Gloria Copeland

* Available in Spanish

From Faith to Faith—A Perpetual Calendar
He Did It All for You
LifeLine Series: Practical Tools for Everyday Needs
- Healing & Wellness: Your 10-Day Spiritual Action Plan
- Your 10-Day Spiritual Action Plan for Complete Financial Breakthrough
- Your 10-Day Spiritual Action Plan for Building Relationships That Last

One Word From God Can Change Your Life

One Word From God Series:
- One Word From God Can Change Your Destiny
- One Word From God Can Change Your Family
- One Word From God Can Change Your Finances
- One Word From God Can Change Your Formula for Success
- One Word From God Can Change Your Health
- One Word From God Can Change Your Nation
- One Word From God Can Change Your Prayer Life
- One Word From God Can Change Your Relationships

Load Up—A Youth Devotional
Over the Edge—A Youth Devotional
Pursuit of His Presence—A Daily Devotional
Pursuit of His Presence—A Perpetual Calendar
Raising Children Without Fear

Other Books Published by KCP

Hello. My Name Is God. by Jeremy Pearsons
John G. Lake—His Life, His Sermons, His Boldness of Faith
Protecting Your Family in Dangerous Times by Kellie Copeland Swisher

The Holiest of All by Andrew Murray
The New Testament in Modern Speech
    by Richard Francis Weymouth
The Rabbi From Burbank by Isidor Zwirn and Bob Owen
Unchained! by Mac Gober

Products Designed for Today's Children and Youth

And Jesus Healed Them All (confession book and CD gift package)
Baby Praise Board Book
Baby Praise Christmas Board Book
Noah's Ark Coloring Book
The Best of *Shout!* Adventure Comics
The *Shout!* Giant Flip Coloring Book
The *Shout!* Joke Book
The *Shout!* Super-Activity Book
Wichita Slim's Campfire Stories

*Commander Kellie and the Superkids*_{SM} Books:

Superkid Academy Children's Church Curriculum
    (DVD/CD curriculum)
- Volume 1—My Father Loves Me!
- Volume 2—The Fruit of the Spirit in You
- Volume 3—The Sweet Life
- Volume 4—Living in THE BLESSING

The SWORD Adventure Book
*Commander Kellie and the Superkids*_{SM}
    Solve-It-Yourself Mysteries
*Commander Kellie and the Superkids*_{SM} Adventure Series:
    Middle Grade Novels by Christopher P.N. Maselli:

    #1 The Mysterious Presence
    #2 The Quest for the Second Half
    #3 Escape From Jungle Island

World Offices
Kenneth Copeland Ministries

For more information about KCM and our products, please
write to the office nearest you:

Kenneth Copeland Ministries
Fort Worth, TX 76192-0001

Kenneth Copeland
Locked Bag 2600
Mansfield Delivery Centre
QUEENSLAND 4122
AUSTRALIA

Kenneth Copeland
Post Office Box 15
BATH
BA1 3XN
U.K.

Kenneth Copeland
Private Bag X 909
FONTAINEBLEAU
2032
REPUBLIC OF
SOUTH AFRICA

Kenneth Copeland
PO Box 3111 STN LCD 1
Langley BC V3A 4R3
CANADA

Kenneth Copeland Ministries
Post Office Box 84
L'VIV 79000
UKRAINE

We're Here for You!

Believer's Voice of Victory Television Broadcast

Join Kenneth and Gloria Copeland and the *Believer's Voice of Victory* broadcasts Monday through Friday and on Sunday each week, and learn how faith in God's Word can take your life from ordinary to extraordinary. This teaching from God's Word is designed to get you where you want to be—*on top!*

You can catch the *Believer's Voice of Victory* broadcast on your local, cable or satellite channels.* Also available 24 hours on webcast at BVOV.TV.

*Check your local listings for times and stations in your area.

Believer's Voice of Victory Magazine

Enjoy inspired teaching and encouragement from Kenneth and Gloria Copeland and guest ministers each month in the *Believer's Voice of Victory* magazine. Also included are real-life testimonies of God's miraculous power and divine intervention in the lives of people just like you!

It's more than just a magazine—it's a ministry.

To receive a FREE subscription to
Believer's Voice of Victory, write to:

Kenneth Copeland Ministries
Fort Worth, TX 76192-0001
Or call:
800-600-7395
(7 a.m.-5 p.m. CT)
Or visit our website at:
www.kcm.org

If you are writing from outside the U.S., please contact the KCM office nearest you. Addresses for all Kenneth Copeland Ministries offices are listed on the previous pages.

- Start putting $ aside for a sitter every month.
- Have faith + believe that God will bring the right person @ the right time.
- Walk by faith, not by sight